Moor Poets

Volume IV

A collection of contemporary poetry

Published by
MOOR POETS

First published in 2018 by Moor Poets
a community of poets based in Devon
moorpoets.weebly.com

Cover picture
Leaving Chinkwell Tor by Anita Reynolds
www.anitareynolds.com

Copyright © 2018 Moor Poets
ISBN 978-0-9551114-3-3

All rights reserved. No part of this book may be reproduced, stored in a retrieval system, or transmitted in any form, or by any means, electronic, mechanical, photocopying, recording or otherwise, or translated into any language, without prior written permission from the publisher, except by a reviewer who may quote brief passages in a review.

All the poets assert their moral right to be identified as the authors of these works, in accordance with the Copyright, Designs and Patents Act 1988.

Design and typesetting by Alwyn Marriage
Printed in Great Britain by imprint digital, Devon

Introduction

Moor Poets is an active creative community that continues to strengthen its influence through a range of activities and events which attract, develop and promote writing talent. This is expressed in a variety of poetic voices and styles which we wanted to celebrate and share in this latest, fourth anthology.

For writers based largely in the rural South-West, with Dartmoor at its heart, at a time of increased pressure on the environment, natural beauty and wildness remain a central source of inspiration. This, however, is always viewed in relation to current and historical human experience as the thing that shapes us.

Offering different perspectives, these poems range in character and tone from serious to playful, dry to exuberant, and in subjects as diverse as *Stick Gathering at Golitha Falls*, *The Fine Art of Body Painting* and *The Woman of Whitehorse Hill*. Yet all draw on the energy of language to celebrate being alive and reflecting on what that means.

We hope you will enjoy this new anthology.

Helen Boyles (Joint Chair of Moor Poets)

Contents

Introduction		
Dartmoor Re-wilding	Virginia Griem	1
Archaeologist	Jenny Hamlett	2
Anti Mass	Graham Burchell	3
Stones	Dawn Bauling	4
Sprawling Stone	Jennie Osborne	5
waiting for it to happen	Simon Millward	6
Dunnabridge Revisited	Ronnie Goodyer	7
Whitsun Song	Angela Howarth	8
Diaries	Mark Haworth-Booth	9
That Apostrophe Thing	Ian Royce Chamberlain	11
Beach Sketch 2	Lucy Pearce	12
Clothes	Jan Nicholls	13
No tears now child	Virginia Griem	14
An Hour across Dartmoor	Simon Williams	15
Red	Julie-ann Rowell	16
Jay's Grave	Susan Jordan	18
Cobber Girl	Julie-ann Rowell	19
The Woman of Whitehorse Hill	Sue Proffitt	20
Passing	David Arnott	22
A Thread	Frances Corkey Thompson	23
The White Lands and the Black	Helen Boyles	24
Unheard	Ian Royce Chamberlain	25
Mother River	Ann Topping	26
Birth Mother	Pat Millner	27
Golden Rhino of Mapungubwe	Pat Millner	28
Fine Art Body Painting	Susan Taylor	29
Seville	Helen Scadding	30
Learning the Ropes	Kerry Priest	31
Mid-afternoon	Kerry Priest	32
Burning Memories	Ann Topping	33
found in translation	Susan Taylor	34
Sea Watcher	Helen Boyles	35
Photos	Angela Howarth	36
Premonition	Rebecca Gethin	37
Walking	Jenna Plewes	38
Let's not go out on this winter day	Ronnie Goodyer	39
Fenland	Jan Nicholls	40

Driving Home	*Jenna Plewes*	41
Midwinter	*Hilary Jupp*	42
Tomorrow	*Jennie Osborne*	43
Stick Gathering at Golitha Falls	*Dawn Bauling*	44
Black Hill	*Rebecca Gethin*	45
Cryptic	*Liz England*	46
Blackbird	*Fenella Montgomery*	47
To the Person on the Bridge	*Sue Proffitt*	48
Grace	*Veronica Aaronson*	50
I never think dark will come	*Susan Jordan*	51
Finding the Light	*Fenella Montgomery*	52
Water Spearwort	*Simon Millward*	53
In the October Garden	*Frances Corkey Thompson*	54
Rock Hard	*Jenny Hamlett*	55
The Fox	*Liz England*	56
In Coach C	*Graham Burchell*	57
Repairing the Roof	*Simon Williams*	58
A Dream of Blue	*Alwyn Marriage*	59
Home-making	*Hilary Jupp*	60
Going Home	*Veronica Aaronson*	61
February Morning	*Helen Scadding*	62
Acknowledgements		63

Dartmoor Re-wilding

Tanglewood, whitewood, spindletrees
by water-runs, birchbark marked by devil's
claw, ash hung with heaven's keys. Here
the bees reign, cockchafer crawls the
undergrowth nudging through the celandine.
Willow warbler cascades his song, sets the
catkins tumbling, while gangs of whitethroats
start a game of chase chase me, and jenny
wren busy in the brush being madam broody
intent on nesting, mouses up the bramble
covered bank. Here the wood is young, sapling
bound, bending each whichway, playful in its
long legged lanky growing, curious in its new
found confidence, ready to sing and dance
with all nature's gifts re-wilding.

Virginia Griem

Archaeologist

He needs only an instant, a slight
turning of the head
      to convince him
he has a listener.

Suddenly he's a runaway train
of information on grooved ware
      and zig-zag lozenges
carved on stone –

the hours spent on his knees
under a fierce sun
      with earth baked hard
impossible to scrape

or with the archaeology
melting in the damp
      as a sea-haar
creeps up his back.

As he speaks we're flooded
by carved stone balls
      and radio-carbon dating
by coloured axe heads and painted pottery.

He's always seeking,
three weeks in his trench
      without a find
always searching, always knowing

he will never know how they spoke
or the colour of their eyes.
      He's digging up
more questions than answers –

radiating success with
the discovery of an axe head –
      that might
add a tiny piece to a jigsaw of lost lives.

Jenny Hamlett

Anti Mass
within the Parish church of Buckfast, Devon, burned in an arson attack, and after the art installation.   Anti Mass (2005), by Cornelia Parker

After an age, one bird does cry out above this place;
one in a rush, passing over. The aftertaste
is a pull of breeze through summer branches,
and me. I'm sat in the ribcage of this gutted,
roasted, whale of a god house,

sat on the side where the bones are shattered,
where all I can see of piety is a Celtic cross –
a crying face, with charcoal fragments,
ash and scorches air-brushed.
The altar, chapels and tracery windows

have taken on wildflowers. Here is air
and shadow patterns; spaces for the unexpected
aerobatics of swallows.

                    Hate far off burned
another church. A creator noticed, saw the black char

as emblematic, ripe for hanging from fine wires,
ripe for holding like an explosion at the midpoint
of its moment, silent, weightless, dark light
that beacons, beckons one
to spear a thought.

Graham Burchell

Inspired by 'La Peri – Poème dansé (not to include the fanfare)', by Dukas

Stones
at Blackingstone Rock

Where you are round
I am flat;
your song
my whistle;
weathered smoothness
to dull my bristle
and angles that are
made suddenly curves.

We are at times
unalike
as leaf and flame

but together
inexplicably
logan stones
balanced perfectly
forever.

Dawn Bauling

Sprawling Stone

I'm the odd one out, neither in the circle
nor out, the merry maiden
whose feet couldn't learn the dance,
tipped me flat on my face in the grass
along with buttercups, cattails, bluebells,
that white lacy one that won't tell me
its name. Good enough company for me.
I've gathered a bit of moss now
and some pretty lichen, something
between yellow, green and blue.
In between. Neither one thing
nor the other. That's me.

I've no desire to join
this circle dance again, or partner
with the tall stone in the middle who leans
at a crazy angle surrounded by campion groupies.

Just three feet away, in the space
between two dancers, there's another
toppled stone, dappled with quartz
and that same pale lichen I wear.
We'll never hold our heads to the sky,
enter the ring. We both know what it's like
to feel the grass growing over,
year by year. Companionship.
Of a sort. It's enough.
Has to be, really.
Same sun, same rain, roots
of grasses running through the soil.
Connections.

Jennie Osborne

waiting for it to happen

two pines dancing
coat-tails trailing
in near symmetry

two pines alone
in the snow leaning
towards each other

never quite touching

Simon Millward

Dunnabridge Revisited
Sonnet in Autumn

Late Autumn, leaning on the wooden gate,
I thought of you in your far Celtic land
and how that first twist of the knife saw fate
so determined that it would lend a hand.
Fresh sunlight and the sanctity of wood,
grass heavy with birthing seed at my feet,
brought back strong memories of days we would
cross over old Dunnabridge Pound and meet.
Sometimes, like children, we'd blow on ripe grass,
or just lie in the flowering meadow,
noticing how quickly long days seemed to pass
until called home by the sun's long shadow.

Here today I'm left with longing and smiles,
thinking of you across the flying miles.

Ronnie Goodyer

Whitsun Song

In May, the white blossoms come:
a foaming of hawthorn, elder, guelder rose
a sprinkle of daisies, cow parsley, rowan.
And if there is a dove, it is white
and if there is a flame, it is the sun
a slow burner, all white heat
or yellow pollen, or tongues of stamens
silently mouthing in one accord
standing high on the tips of their roots
reaching into the air a petalled hand
to catch the fire descending into
a wild consummation of seed.

And if we have a dove, it is breath in bone.
And if we have a flame, it is heart beat,
a phoenix burner, molten heat.
And if there is a word, it is spoken
from the tips of our roots, raising seed,
uttering syllables of sap into light
with one accord blossomed into deed.

Angela Howarth

Diaries
after an image by Walter Benjamin

I have so many, piled up in my desk's
recesses, going back some twenty years.
They're very useful too, if someone asks
about, say, when a family gathering was
or when we had the boiler serviced, when
exactly we were on that holiday,
this or that meeting, medical appointments –
no space for stuff I fool with on most days.
Sometimes I keep a journal and write up
those other things we do – around the garden,
the wild life seen, the films, our daughters, friendships,
local and national politics, our reading.
But neither diary nor journal record
how minutes fell like snowflakes. Not a word.

Mark Haworth-Booth

Ground Nesting Birds of the Dartmoor Uplands

A man in the audience raises his hand
and – using a heavily-freighted word –
asks if badgers are a problem for the birds.

To which the doctoral student from Holland replies:

no, crows and foxes are major problems,
not the badgers – but the greatest decimator
of Dartmoor birds is Dartmoor weather.

Mark Haworth-Booth

That Apostrophe Thing

There's a lonely outcrop below Buckland-in-the-Moor,
shown on early OS maps as Lovers Leap...

Is it possible to not imagine
how it got its name
Lovers Leap?

A rocky ledge high above the Dart
and a love-lorn Romeo – or Juliet –
watching all that water rushing past
and then...

Can you taste the passion, feel the pain?
Listen for the scream, thud, splash

       the sudden silence.

Anyway — this Lovers Leap,
what's it doing out there, miles from anywhere?

Why would a love-lorn Romeo – or Juliet –
go that far? Along the way they would have missed
a dozen opportunities for jumping, drowning
or just lying down to freeze to death.

And something else – the lack of an apostrophe.
So Lovers Leap must be a statement, present tense.
Surely not – we'd hear about it.

We need punctuation!
Was it Romeo, or Juliet – or both of them?
How many lovers leapt?

Ian Royce Chamberlain

Beach Sketch 2

Bleached, desert dry
unslakeable thirst
balanced against each other's
smoothness, constantly shifting
edges knocked off by eons

of tumbling together, rubbing along
small dark spaces in between
fill with undertows shwoosh
and drag

A giant scattered
slumbering stone wall
blanket
heaved across the beach
each tidal pull

lying drily still
calling out to the sea
"Give us your green wetness."

Lucy Pearce

Clothes

I avoided your glove on the motorway,
a cupped hand buffeted by the stream of cars.

You keep returning,
a movement in the corner of my eye –

your clothes lift and fall on the line –

they'll stay there bleaching and fraying
as your emptiness falls apart.

I place my blouse over your jacket,
my jersey on your folded shirt.

Jan Nicholls

No tears now child as you lie so quiet
Under 'An Act for Burying in Woollen onely' brought in by Parliament to protect the English wool trade in 1666, all burials without a woollen shroud will be subject to a fine of £5.

I shall spin you a yarn that will make your shroud
I shall gather the wool from a moorland field
Strand by strand from the gorse and the mire
Wash it pure in the peat stained stream
Teasel it soft white as a cloud

I shall weave the cloth with scraps of the land
Build me a loom from a Wistman's tree
Whisper the shuttle against the warp
Weave it fine as the curl at your brow

I shall spin you a yarn that will make your shroud
Swaddle you tight and lay you down
Deep in the earth to keep you warm
Get it writ clear you are buried in wool
Safe in the book for all to see

No tears now child as you lie so quiet
The wool is gathered the yarn is spun
Woven as light as a night moth wing
And out in the cold a curlew calls
You are buried in wool – in wool – in wool

Virginia Griem

An Hour across Dartmoor

Sheep fade up behind their sapphire eyes,
with lambs not old enough to know
sheep stand their ground.

A calf wanders into the dark
around our lights, like an exit stage left
in a silent, Balinese mime.

Bat and owl are so brief
a quick stall turn and a sweep
between trees is their parting.

Ponies confirm their freedom
to common graze the verge
and block the carriageway at night.

Only the hare, pitched forward
like a dragster on a burnout,
is rarity, daring to lollop.

Simon Williams

Red

Devon red, sea-wise red if cliffs crumble
looks like blood-spill of some great mammal,
red cries no haven if you fall short.

Mariner looks for red on a skyline
dots of light, keep to the right
steer your boat's hemline steeped

in the kettle of dark, black the only opposite
to red – they understand each other,
black corrects, simplifies, red trumpets

keep right forget other hues, determinations
pay attention to what counts
red lamb leg of rock, a bleed high up,

the land's sheath pierced, red
doesn't want to blend. See the crimson sheep
on the cliff? Even the sea's overwhelmed.

Julie-ann Rowell

A Psalm for the Women who Worked on the Land

A psalm for the women who worked on the land,
who didn't have a choice,
living in the middle of nowhere,
didn't want to work as a cleaner for the farmer's wife,
so instead went out every morning
to bend their backs in fields.

A psalm for Dorothy
in her Land Army overalls,
faded and patched,
who'd never married,
a penknife in her top pocket
to peel the apples.

A psalm for Vera,
hair in a headscarf,
needed the morning tea break
before we started,
when the December days were short,
stopping for a fag, catching us up.

Yes, a psalm for the women,
hardworking, cheerfully uncomplaining,
sat in a cold hut to eat sandwiches,
no toilet, no tap to wash hands,
at the edge of a muddy field
reeking of rotting sprouts.

A psalm for Mrs Payne
who gave me a bunch of Mock Orange
for my wedding bouquet,
didn't like being called by her first name,
handing round a white paper bag of "winter mixture"
to keep us going through the dreary afternoons.

A psalm for my young self,
the one who got away.

Sally Willow

Jay's Grave

I've tried to sleep for more than a hundred years
in this grass triangle, juddered by cars,
prodded by sheep feet, explained by walkers
who know me only as a landmark on a map.

My softened bones are sunk into dark peat
juicy with streams and urine and trapped rain.
My flesh melts through the mulch of leaves;
atoms of my blood infuse the heather.

Once I placed lilies in tall vases on the altar
of others' pleasure. Now they bring me
buttercups, campion, rosebay willow-herb,
flowers I wouldn't have given a second look.

This apron-shaped bed won't let me forget
the service I bore, doing always for them
what no-one did for me. He made me into
the silent vessel for all his consequences.

They denied me my rest where others lie
secure in their righteousness. They left me here,
the tilted hills behind me and a bracken field,
alone with the wide moor and the cradling sky.

Susan Jordan

According to Dartmoor legend the roadside grave is that of a young woman, Kitty Jay, who became pregnant and committed suicide. I have imagined she was a servant, although I don't think she was.

Cobber Girl

Raising the little hammer to the hunk of ore,
she breaks the copper into pieces for the bucker,

her hands inside gloves bought from the chapman
hoping to keep skin decent, face shaded by a gook.

No man she knows can buy her life and raise it
higher than the chimneystack of the engine house,

still, she cares for her looks, bal maiden or no.
Hates the wind. Hates the rain. Water is wetter here

her mother once said. Now Ma is in her grave
at Portreath, twenty years grinding cobbed ore

into powder for packing. It's a great business,
the owners told them, you can build a life here.

Bring your children to shovel and haul, and all
will reap the sun in the coinage of copper

that lines the bellies of ships, makes bronze and brass –
it's a stable living, what else would you do

in this Cornish tip? Cobber girl chips on, cracks and splits.
Her life a handbarrow of pebbles too heavy to lift.

Julie-ann Rowell

gook: hood made of cardboard

The Woman of Whitehorse Hill

In August 2011, a granite kist was excavated on Whitehorse Hill, north Dartmoor. The peat bog that had hidden it was eroding and the west stone fell outwards, exposing the kist. The peat had protected what was found inside: the cremated remains of a young woman laid on an animal pelt. The remains are over 4000 years old.

The stones have been singing to me for as long as I can remember
their cracks and edges rubbing against each other slowly.

I sensed the peat stretching itself around us
bringing that black that is all root – matted bones
choked throats – still the stones sang, indifferent.

I did not mind the deeper dark,
felt the soft shift of my dust on your pelt, my beloved.

I came with beads, the ash bride.
Amber like your eyes – the resinous heat of your eyes –
two of them on my wrist, and shale, glint-cold like the rivers.

This was my gift. You would see me
on the other side of the fire
dressed for the journey.

The dark took us further than I could have dreamed.

Then change came. Cold.
Rain coming in slantways and something else, sharp, so sweet –
heather, honey of gorse, vinegar of moor grass –
and the singing stopped.

Now I hear buzzards keening above.
You hear it too, I know. I feel you stir.

Something has disturbed our final coupling.
I was warm, the fire's heat still inside me –
now blown open –

voices.

Something is happening to us.
I am leaving the stones behind

aghast in air –
they finger me   finger you
separating   what is conjoined

the eyes of my beads shriek – they cannot know
as they open my ceremonial bag
what is being released –

we are lifted up – a soft dust, a scrape of fur.
Soft dust. Scrape of fur.

The sky falls through us.

Sue Proffitt

Passing
for Sara, hill farmer, potter, mother, died untimely November 2015

The ewe in passing leaves a tuft of wool
tangled on barbwire. The stream in passing
caresses curves in silt, smoothes jagged stones
into speckled eggs. The ferns in passing

snare sunbeams into peat that may one day
blaze again, fossilised sunlight set free.
The potter with each pass spins and smoothes wet clay
hands curved around what's yet unborn, and sees

an everyday chalice. Now she herself has passed
leaving tangled memory, jagged pain,
the slow smoulder of loss and love. Ourselves
rough earthenware crocks, who long again
for the banked up fire to blaze and dance and roar
and the best wine yet, that's kept till last, be poured.

David Arnott

A Thread

Her brother fell in the dark race for the boat.
The child made it on board, her eyes and mind
closed to further cruelty. A sailor,
in a kind of fondness, kept her, sold her
in Cork City for a copper coin.

They took her, wild and dumb, to the place
of Huguenots, her own people, strangers
grown stranger here, even to themselves.
Fearful and fatigued, they had landed
the year before, bringing with them nothing
but what was lodged in their hands and heads –
the skills of trade, and systems of production.
The good people of Ireland (and the bad),
seeing no gain in adding pain to sorrow,
had offered to the protestant-strangers refuge
of basic sort – food and a roof – and left them.

The child, though warmed and fed, would not speak
all her first Irish winter. Then, late in Spring,
a flower bloomed, the colour of summer sky.
She touched it with, she saw, her mother's hand,
recalled the red fists that tugged the stalks,
how maman called the men and boys to heave
the stinking, retted fibres from the dam.
She felt the rhythmic grip that scutched the shive.
Escousser, she said aloud. *Escousse comme ça.*
Her skinny arms folded as maman's would
in satisfaction when they'd laid the last
lengths of linen out in the sun to bleach
on fields almost as green as these around.

Frances Corkey Thompson

Huguenot refugees brought their skills to the Irish linen industry.
Escousser: old French, to scrutch. Scrutching is a step in the procesing of flax into linen,

The White Lands and the Black

Stark on the summit,
dark on the bleached bent of the moor,
the gibbet is a rune
scored on the sky's blank.
Chains where a body hung
from its outstretched arm,
drip in the mist,
anchored foot rusts in the peat.
The angle of its one eye
holds the vastnesses,
funnels mind's imaginings
into the white land, the black,
the acid and the sand of heights and deeps,
lives lapped in earth and sky,
plans hatched in the secret shafts
of consciousness.

The crumbled Saxon cross beneath
may try to shame the memory,
cannot erase the signature
of violence and punishment, some half-
remembered tale of rivalry or bitterness,
a struggle and a smothered cry,
the fatal strike, abandoned corpse
and felon struggling to his sentence
through the slow clutch of the bog,
the long reach of the law.

We are warned: don't stumble here,
stray from the lighted path;
the place will spill you into emptiness,
fold you in its white breath,
tip you and tilt you,
float you on the curlew's keening
far to the sliding edge.

Helen Boyles

Unheard

I speak for Flanders Field
for grit and clay, ditch and canal.
I speak for the soil seeded with fury,
with shell case and bullet
offal and bone. I speak
for the forest of chestnut and oak
and the crashing of giants.

I speak for the toad in the gulley
fieldmouse and cricket, blackbird and thrush
for the bee at the splintered hive.
I speak for the rifled pig
the maggoted carcass of cow
the sugar beet crop in a pulp of cratered waste
and the churn with its shrapnel slash.

I speak for the poisoned ponds
for the stifled gills of milk-eyed pike and crayfish killed
by the oily piss of fighting machines.
I speak with a tunnel of fire for a throat
and a mustard of mud in my lungs.
When the listening begins
the poppies will speak for themselves.

Ian Royce Chamberlain

Mother River

Below the weir, she contemplates the sky
impressed on her liquid-silver skin,
the brownish crowns, the cloud-pink dusk
and the moon's boldfaced wink.

She carries confetti of summer feasts,
echoes of teenage throbs and pasted grins
cloaked in a pungent scent, on her banks
muddied by damp air and spore dust.

And when the boy whose mind unclipped
on ketamine falls in, she wraps a mantle
around him, licks his salty sweat
and though he flaps and fidgets like a fledgling,

she cuddles and soothes, pulls his limbs beyond
the whirlpools by the bridge's arch,
where she lays him under the canopy closure.

As she hears the last beat sink,
she roars out loud
beneath the sky's glazed eye.

Ann Topping

Birth Mother

The reeds where she left me
were bronze and golden.
So were the two
small frantic dupes
toiling all summer
to feed me till I fledged.

As the water stilled
its mirror showed
my true colours,
my silver stripes,
my slate grey throat.
We could not be kin.

But she'd left me only
my heart's dark magnet
fixed on the south,
four thousand miles
of trackless sky
to navigate alone.

She must be here somewhere.
The huge green leaves
are bewildering,
a wet curtain
behind the dripping flowers.
I call from branch to branch.
       How could you, could you, could you?

Pat Millner

Golden Rhino of Mapungubwe

The sculptor dreamed you
out of sunlight,
acacia scent
and your horned shadow
on the winter grass,
to keep the nightmares
from a dead king.

They buried you again,
hurriedly next time,
 covering your story
like a hornless corpse
before the vultures
could spread it
to the eavesdropping sky.

But you charge head down
out of the grave
scattering white lies,
uprooting history
like a smashed baobab,
and skid to a halt
your shining hide ablaze.

Pat Millner

Note: *The rhino was excavated from a thirteenth century royal grave in Limpopo Province South Africa in 1932 and swiftly consigned to a university basement because it failed to fit the current narrative of 'primitive' societies. It is now a treasured work of art.*

Fine Art Body Painting
after the work of Johannes Stoetter

Paint me frog, paint me shine, paint me liquid green,
emblazon the storms of a rainforest onto my skin.
Catch me red-handed, red-footed and just poised
to leap into some starry bromeliad pool,
where the water is sweet as pineapple juice.

Paint me wolf, paint me howl, paint my head as the start
of the wild. Get me stretching for what I was born to be …
sharp-scented by nature and able to place the optimum
stress on my body for meaningful strength in every move,
so I equal challenges in my way – however they appear.

Paint me fish, give me fins in surprising places, not just
for my hands, but the parts which are harder to reach.
Tickle me into all kinds of heavenly blue for my scales.
I am ready to breathe in water as well as familiar air.
This sapphire-bright planet tips me a come-to-play wink.

Paint me chameleon, for here is the best most believable part;
it takes two, at least, who are able to share the spectrum
of colours, the rainbow nation of skin to kindred skin.
Paint me ladybird, tiger, grasshopper, whale,
paint me crow, paint me crab, paint my craving for life.

Susan Taylor

Seville

I am turning into somebody else –
somebody who makes marmalade.

Somebody who rolls a cool thick Seville
against her cheek
breathing in the scent of Spain
in the dusk of Devon.

Somebody who cuts thin peel
skimming golden froth
from amber soup
in a January kitchen.

When did this happen?
Watching the teaspoon for the set,
boiling the jars,
writing tidy labels.

I should be wearing
a white dress
gazing up through blossom
at a Spanish blue sky

biting into olive flesh
and running my fingers
along red walls
warm with secrets

instead of lining up
nine jars of sun.

Helen Scadding

Learning the Ropes

My ebay seller had no teeth in
when I got to the bungalow.

She demonstrated teddies
every neat stitch identical,

got the Singer machine nattering
showed me the ropes. So easy

for her, so hard for me this
regularity, this hushed life

in a moorland town with all the
power of a sewing machine

totally under her control
while the stitches only
      run
         away from me.

Kerry Priest

Mid-afternoon

I rollerskate in
but am soon seduced
into the fog-slow unrolling
of a day stretched out and sleepy in front of your black and
white telly.

Always drawn
to the hearth and its tracklements,
lulled orange by the coals, I stay to see
the little couple come out the clock as the barometer clicks to
rain.

Afternoons
drip by, awaiting
kettle whistle, ice-cream van chime
waiting for you to leave the room so I can shake the bell in the
brass lady's dress.

You shake the tin
of Nestles for three languid minutes,
ease off the lid with liver-spotted hands
and sliding the cream over Coop pear or peach halves, smile at
me

and these afternoons last forever
until they don't.

Kerry Priest

Burning Memories

My fingers dig in the sand,
peer under the baby skin of pebbles
searching for child-things. All gone,

Mother said, eyes shifting
to the dipping sun. It unzipped a purple tongue
onto the swallowing waves. Whoosh,

she whispered to the flame
as it blistered our family pictures
and the wind sent

a filigree of memories
flying like sea foam.

Ann Topping

found in translation

before 针灸
mind is willow in wind; a long-haired acrobat.
the pond ruffles and agitates as leafy leader fronds
skim the surface, then sometimes skip, dip and dishevel
rain lines embroiled further and further in ripples.
wood and water meet.
during zhēnjiǔ
mindful of depth, body of water stills,
resonant to willow wands pinned gently in.
it's a different tingle from each tip of silver,
as meniscus dimples at flashpoints of touch.
water and metal bridge.
after acupuncture
the old willow mind throws out her thousands
of tendril trails into a swirling circle. swallows, come
dance in the intermittent rain's bows, dipping in flight,
to stitch razzle dazzle through the pond's mirroring.
earth and fire embrace

Susan Taylor

Sea Watcher

We read the sea again
this morning, early, on the height,
for dolphin signatures.
His blue eyes set in weathered skin
see more than most, trained
to the scribble on the waves,
the serif flourish, plunging stroke,
ruffle of the shifting tides,
the textures, shadows, light.
Signs yield
to his patient deciphering.
Rooted in stillness
he holds the horizon line,
the middle distance, far and near,
holds time in a bowl
without spilling.

Helen Boyles

Photos

There, crouched in front of our little house
your sunhat hides your eyes
light glints off newly washed windows
my reflection, broken by glazing bars
presses down on the button, click
a tiny whirr like a wheel beginning to spin.

And this one, taken sideways, unaware
of the way my shadow overlays yours
across the daisied lawn. The navy shirt
you chose to wear to the clinic
looks black in such harsh August light
glaring through the hush of your news.

Now I am in the picture, unsure
of how to compose myself in focus
as the automatic shutter exposes
a million shades of that moment
you and I look down at our hands
scanning for life-lines.

Angela Howarth

Premonition

A light still operates inside
the phone box with its red paint
flaking off the grid of panes.

A corona of moths searches
for an entrance. Inside, a shroud
of cobwebs embodies the space,

like a sketch of someone
stood waiting for an incoming call –
but the receiver dangles

on its cord, encased in web,
and no voice asks again and again
for a word with the spiders.

Rebecca Gethin

Walking

A path meanders walnut groves,
orchards of cherry, peach and plum,
skirts meadows knee-high in ox-eye daisies,
clover and forget-me-nots, heaves itself
up hillsides blowsy with blossom, loud
with the bubbling song of nightingales.

Far below, a river snakes in and out of sight
trees smother the sky, leaves rustle with rain
cuckoos call, tedious as dripping taps,
in slime-green pools frogs
gargle their muddy throats.

We walk, boots slithery with wet, a pace set by
centuries of travellers, our days tuned to the
rhythm of our steps, within a breathing space
that opens boundaries, closes behind our backs
leaving no trace.

Jenna Plewes

Let's not go out on this winter day

Let's not go out on this winter day,
the wind is shouting at the walls,
the fire won't take that long to catch,
the softness of the sofa calls.

Let's not go out on this winter day,
let's both hold still and think of ways
to travel worlds inside our heads,
refuse the places winter stays.

Let's walk through books, let's walk through poems,
visit Fern Hill and Dover Beach;
to Yeats' Lake Isle of Innisfree,
Frost's America, Homer's Greece.

Let's drink too much and let's laugh too loud
let's find what sheer indulgence brings;
Let's clink our glasses while we can
and catch each other's hiccupping!

Then let our music resound from rooms,
as we struggle to sing as one,
Strawberry Fields, Forever Young,
Redemption Song, Here Comes The Sun.

Let's not go out on this winter day
but well before the flames expire,
let's sink into each other's arms,
make love before our winter fire.

Ronnie Goodyer

Fenland

He drives me through sunlight
across black ploughed fields,
clouds defining the distance.
I feel like an empty piece of clothing
that no longer has any shape
and ask him if I seem different.
He plays me his favourite music –
a violin, recorder and viol,
yearning to make a jig –
then he opens the windows
and I'm lifted out
and blown across the fens
with nothing to stop me.

Jan Nicholls

Driving Home

The road is reeling him in
mile after mile after mile,
pulling him through dark waters.

Needlefish aim for his eyes,
shoal after shoal hit the glass,
he stares ahead, unblinking,

feels the line tighten, then slacken;
the hook deep in his gut holds.
He lets the night stream past,

conjures her voice, smell of her skin,
paper-thin feel of her fingers,
replays their wordless conversation.

Wipers click a mantra in his head,
the tug and tear of severing
is still to come.

Jenna Plewes

Midwinter

A redshank's call
lifts the gaze
to a sight of spindle tree

bare
but for its fruit

a blow
to the senses
on this drab day

when heads are crooked
against the chill

and thoughts turned inwards
are stunned
to look outside themselves

at these small silken parcels
neon pink
in the dun of winter

Hilary Jupp

Tomorrow

The phone rings, and you'd think there'd be a sense
of knife about to slice your life in two.
It's not like that at all. I have a shoe
half on, I'm leaving soon. There's no pretence
of normal in her voice. It's Peter, he's ...
the story dribbles out. How she'd got home
from holiday and found ... I grasp the phone.
I spoke to him last night, he called me. She's
not making sense. She's talking about blood
and mattresses. He's only fifty-nine.
The house booms silence once she's off the line.
I crave a hug, a hand, go down the road,
find friends. Can't make it real, can't say a word.
Not yet. Tomorrow, yes, that's when I heard.

Jennie Osborne

Stick gathering at Golitha Falls

If every stick or stone
in my bag and boot
on this unexceptional day
had a walk attached,
all valley tied, fell studded
plain or plimsoll,
even barefoot tired,
I would have enough.
They would be my wood,
my hedge and beach,
my cottage hearth beside,
each one turned
and seasoned by a hand,
a paw, a storm,
a child or tide;
a better gathering tied
under the chiselled hazel
lintel of my heart
unbriared.

Dawn Bauling

Black Hill

I arrived by the other path
along the cliffs, through the woods
and met my last year self
taking the same photos –
Gribbin Head,The Lizard,
the difference being the snow
of blackthorn blossom, the cold wind
of spring. That was before a diagnosis,
then waiting rooms, waiting weeks.
This time there was less of me
and with more understanding
of the early campion, the chiff chaff
repeating its call, the wonder
that I'd made it here at all.

Rebecca Gethin

Cryptic

A puzzle of
frost encrusted leaves
a jigsaw of decay
crunches under boots.

Above, white noise,
the river's cold blood
coursing though
black veins.

Paint brush green moss
crumpled into wounds
of dying branches.

A black dog weaves
water into a rainbow
chasing sticks.

Sunlight sparks
white spume,
another peace
is broken.

Mist rises through trees
yellow leaves
summer lies
shattered on the rocks.

Liz England

Blackbird

I was standing on the brink of black, balancing.
Perhaps we ought to stop the drugs, they said.
Your body isn't coping. They couldn't tell me
if it had been worth the trip, or not.

One morning I woke to a sound so clear, it was purer
than thought and as liquid as a cool, calm pond.
Notes so precious I wanted to wear them as earrings.
And there he was, calling from a weeping willow
opening the day, inviting me to step inside.

Each day he returned and took his stage
singing me back into summer
spilling orange
slowly painting the darkness bright
until I saw that even black is filled with colour.

Fenella Montgomery

To the Person on the Bridge

The bridge is closed off, my sister says.
Two fire engines, three police cars and an ambulance.
Probably a suicide. Clicks off her phone.

We are replete from a restaurant
where bunches of baubles
hung above us like enormous grapes.

Sparkling wine, reminiscences passed
back and forth like a soft gift between us
while outside the drizzle fell

on a river souped in mist – already swollen
–   and the damp clings to your skin
as you stand clutching wet stone,

its cold hardness the only solid.
Beneath, a thick shine of water
blotted in lights.

It's as if I see you as we drive home
wonder why there wasn't a point
when my fork missed

its target or a glass   slipped,
smashed,
something happened inside,

a caught breath,
a sudden lurch
downwards in my gut,

some kind of knowing
that while we stroked the shining threads
of our shared story

a mile away
yours was balled up
in your wet fist

dropped like a stone.

Sue Proffitt

Grace

Sometimes
it's difficult
to have faith
that the dark moon
will shine full-faced again.

Then in the jumble
of petrol pumps,
concrete, lines of lorries,
a full moon beams,
oozes brightness,
reminds those listening
that tides breathe
even on the blackest night.

Veronica Aaronson

I never think dark will come

all I am is pulse and heave
altered each moment by light

day is slow to warm me

I know the sun's wide road
only when my surface tingles
with glitter points that flash and spark

deep down I am always dark

clouds shade me through green and beyond
arrows of rain darken me before night
so I lose the sun without finding the moon

the fade of day covers me in grey gauze
I bask in the sweet fire that lingers over me

sometimes light slopes away in secret
stealing my warmth   blinding me to myself
till all I know is my own movement

I never think light will return

Susan Jordan

Finding the Light

Inside the dark shed, rhubarb is growing
and only candlelight lets you see
bulbous heads on slim pink stalks.

A soft yellow glow makes you want to whisper
as if the rhubarb is sleeping in its nursery bed
watched over by a hundred nightlights.

If you crouch down and listen carefully
every now and then you'll hear a crack
like popping corn, as a bud breaks open.

This rhubarb, earthy and sweet
is less forced than invited, to reach up
through the silent candlelit vigil
leaves unfurling to receive communion
like grateful prayer hands.

Fenella Montgomery

Water Spearwort

Down the throat of the waterfall
the torrents sluice the earth clean pouring
all ways into a cauldron with such a frenzy
of power that causes only chaos
yet finds a way out into one current

while high on the edge of a mossy rock
spearwort leans over, maybe to see
how deep it is or wash its petals
in the spray, or perhaps just buffeted
there by a natural force
then finds there is no way back

so, before all this white fury – leaves, stalk,
and a yellow flower opened out like a tiny
parachute at the end of the curve.

Simon Millward

In the October Garden

Suddenly unbraced, her bodywork
trailed in swathes, its patina
lost to shades of grief.
'Clearances' uttered itself.
Some words will not be unforged.

Her silk can outface bullets,
out-tonnage steel, span rivers
like the web of a female architect.
She is not weaving, but building.
Welding, annealing, turning.

She plumbed the face of the air.
A finger caught her invisible chain
and wafted her to the wall
She unfurled. Sunlight
plated her eight busy arms.

Frances Corkey Thompson

Rock Hard
below Steeperton Tor

Like taking a test
    for peripheral vision
the corner of my eye fastens
on a brownish-black dot

Sunlight in my face
The rock grows closer
    larger   shifts itself
from dot to lump

It's not quite granite
more of an erratic
yet no glaciers have travelled
    this far south

    A beautiful day
almond-coloured clouds
above the ford
a light wind stirring

Close now   the rock has sprouted
    dark brown hair
A sweet-sick smell
A leg stretched out stiff in mid-air

Gone the supple movement
of pastern and fetlock
    Where's the soft whicker
of greeting   the gentle snuffling

of velvet lips in the palm of my hand

Jenny Hamlett

The Fox

a round red centre, like a full stop,
a bull's eye encircled by the red fur
splayed out and silent in the grass
nose pointing north; the buzzard
indignant on the fence post, her meal
disturbed by our noisy 4x4
bouncing across mud and tussocks;
her partner already a speck
against the clouds, more circumspect
but poised to return to the feast.

Another field, another fox
alert but oblivious
skitters around, nose down,
fixed on the scent of prey;
firebrand of energy,
a heat seeking missile
sharing with us the spark
of single-mindedness.

Liz England

In Coach C

tucked against that sensible shoe,
that stockinged leg. It's as black
as the stomach walls of dragonfish,
except when the sun finds a way,
glances it with passing patterns
and picks out the gold of zip teeth.
There it hunkers, well fed, gaping,
exhaling old lady leather, scented
tissues, lip balm, coin and ticket.

Graham Burchell

Repairing the Roof

Two things you should know:
on Dartmoor we make do and mend –
don't spend when we can bodge it –
and that she and I are poets.

So when the waved asbestos roof
above our kitchen leaked in the rain
and drops fell on the floor
in the torrential showers of early March,

we found a plastic document wallet,
slid it between two of the corrugated panels
and called it near enough;
the rain slid down towards the gutter.

A year on and the drips are back,
reflection of the steady grey that sweeps up
from the Lizard. In the attic
our repair has come adrift.

We replace the plastic wallet
with a cheery red one, notice that the old,
bedraggled patch is half eaten
by snails. The postman says

they had to put a draft excluder
in the postbox to stop the snails eating
stamps off mailed letters.
Our cobbled roof repair must look delicious.

Simon Williams

A Dream of Blue

In May a sea of blossoms in the woods
bathed our eyes in blue, while in the garden
spikes reached up towards a matching sky
and intricate bells swelled and frilled around
their delicate pale stamens.

Arriving on high moorland in a June night's
fading light, the detail of the flora on the ground
around was bleached of colour, scents
swept away by wind. We slept.

Woken by skylarks, we looked out
to find our van embraced by tiny bluebells
pushing through coarse grass and bracken stalks,
nodding their agreement to the day.

Alwyn Marriage

Home-making

In lath and plaster walls
you found cattle bones,
scavenged, then dragged indoors
from the lean-to workshop
that had once been

the village slaughterhouse:
beams propped,
slates concave,
gambrels block and tackle
laid aside.

You took it down
slate by slate,
recut and rebuilt
stone by stone.

In the old parlour-post-office
joists and stairs,
frames and doors
riddled with worm.
You saw to it all.

From the dairy
you raised slate slabs,
stacked them outdoors
where ribwort plantain
and buttercup sprang between,

then shovelled out underlying earth.
We helped barrow it down
our one hundred and sixty foot
allotted ground,
spread it towards

the old stooped apple tree.
Bone tired we climbed
our makeshift ladder
to effortless sleep.

Hilary Jupp

Going Home

On waking, I look across the sound.
The mainland is fog-bound, unknowable.

Suitcase packed, I stand staring out to sea.
A silver streak of light lands on water,
leaches into slate –
three hundred million white birds
are readying themselves for flight
over and over, without taking off,
as if they're not sure whether to risk
journeying home.

Then, only then, I recognise
the source of my own stirring.

Veronica Aaronson

February Morning

The dawn sun stretches behind black oaks
stroking apple trees blanketed in lichen.

The washed grass shakes itself clean.
The pond breathes, yawning with spawn.

The falling moon lights up the chimney's face
as it rises from the thatch.

And I steam against the cold wall
sipping my small piece of the morning.

Helen Scadding

Acknowledgements

'Archaeologist' by Jenny Hamlett was published in *Artemis*, November 2017
'Anti-Mass' by Graham Burchell was runner-up in the *BBC Proms poetry competition* 2016
'Stones' and 'Stick Gathering at Golitha Falls' by Dawn Bauling were published in *Reach Poetry* and in *Shippen* (Indigo Dreams 2014)
'waiting for it to happen' and 'Water Spearwort' by Simon Millward were published in *An Invitation* (The Write Factor 2015)
'Dunnabridge Revisited' and 'Let's not go out on this winter day' by Ronnie Goodyer were published in Indigo Dreams (*bluechrome* 2003)
'Whitsun Song' by Angela Howarth was published in *Other Poetry*, 2000
'Photos' by Angela Howarth was published in *Orbis* (2005)
'Diaries' by Mark Haworth-Booth was published in *Acumen*, January 2017
'No tears now child as you lie so quiet' by Virginia Griem was published in *Threads* Exeter Poetry Festival (2015)
'Jay's Grave' by Susan Jordan was published in *The Chronicles of Eve* (Paper Swans Press 2016)
'The Woman of Whitehorse Hill' by Sue Proffitt won first prize in the *Teignmouth Poetry Festival competition* 2017
'A Thread' by Frances Corkey Thompson won 2nd prize in the *Belfast Poems for Solidarity competition* 2017
'Unheard' by Ian Chamberlain was published by *ExCite Poetry* (2014), and in *Vertigo & Beeswax*, Oversteps Books 2017
'Seville' by Helen Scadding was published in *Exclamation*. Exeter University (June 2017)

'Premonition' by Rebecca Gethin was published in *Prole*, 2016
'Black Hill' by Rebecca Gethin was published in *Ink, Sweat and Tears*, 2017
'Grace' by Veronica Aaronson was published in *Dawntreader*, Winter 2016
'Walking' by Jenna Plewes was published in *Reach Poetry*, 2017
'Driving Home' by Jenna Plewes won first prize in the *Settle Sessions competition* 2017
'Tomorrow' by Jennie Osborne won the *Ware Sonnet Prize* 2016
'A dream of blue' by Alwyn Marriage was published in *Notes from a Camper van*, Bellhouse Books 2014

Moor Poets would like to thank Alwyn Marriage for designing and typesetting the book.